IS NUCLEAR ENERGY SAFE?
NUCLEAR ENERGY AND FISSION

PHYSICS 7TH GRADE
CHILDREN'S PHYSICS BOOKS

Speedy Publishing LLC
40 E. Main St. #1156
Newark, DE 19711
www.speedypublishing.com
Copyright 2017

In this book, we're going to talk about Nuclear Energy and whether it's safe or not. So, let's get right to it!

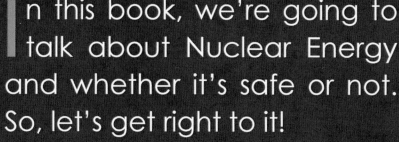
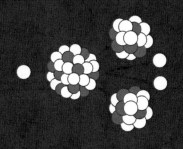

WHAT ARE ATOMS?

In order to understand nuclear energy, you need to know a little about the nature of matter. All the objects that we see in our daily life are made up of matter. Atoms are the "building blocks" of that matter.

We can't see atoms but all the matter in the universe is composed of atoms. Atoms cannot be seen with the naked eye.

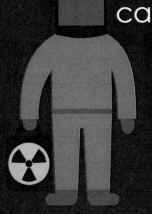

ATOM

At the beginning, scientists thought that atoms were the smallest units of matter, but it was discovered that atoms are made up of subatomic particles called electrons, as well as protons, and neutrons.

SCIENTIST LOOKING
THROUGH A MICROSCOPE

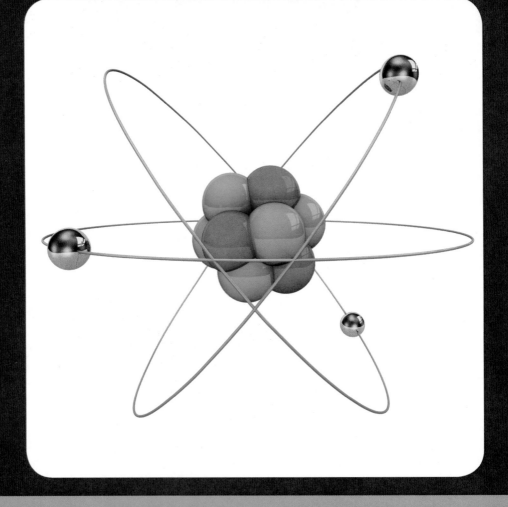

ATOM WITH GOLDEN ELECTRONS, PURPLE PROTONS AND GREEN NEUTRONS

Protons have a charge that is positive. Electrons have a charge that is negative and neutrons are neutral and have no charge. Neutrons and protons are made up of even tinier particles called quarks.

There is also a type of subatomic particle called a neutrino. It is similar to an electron, but it doesn't have any charge. Neutrinos are created during nuclear reactions.

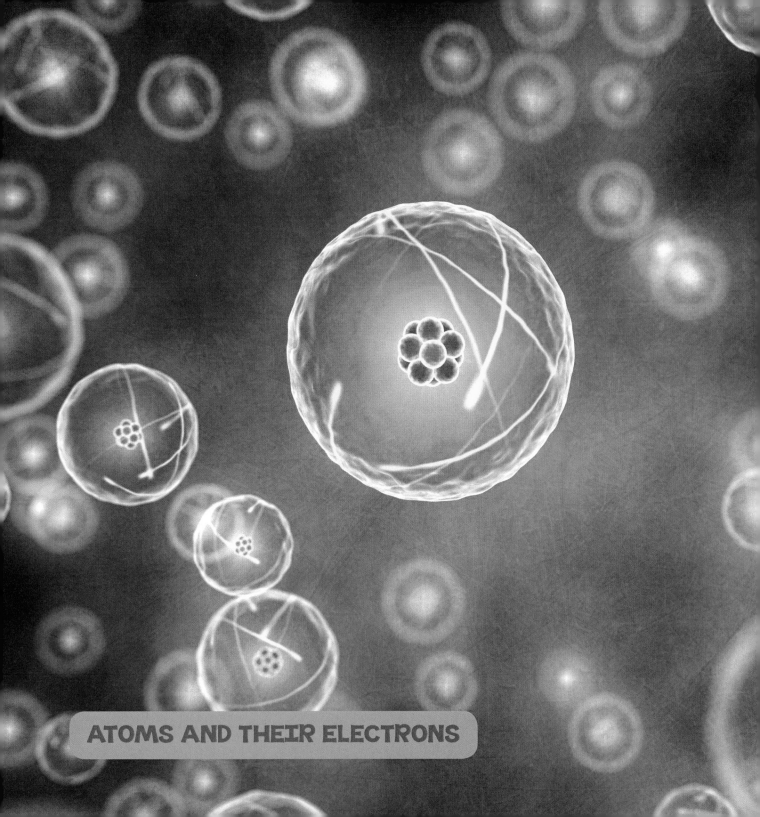

ATOMS AND THEIR ELECTRONS

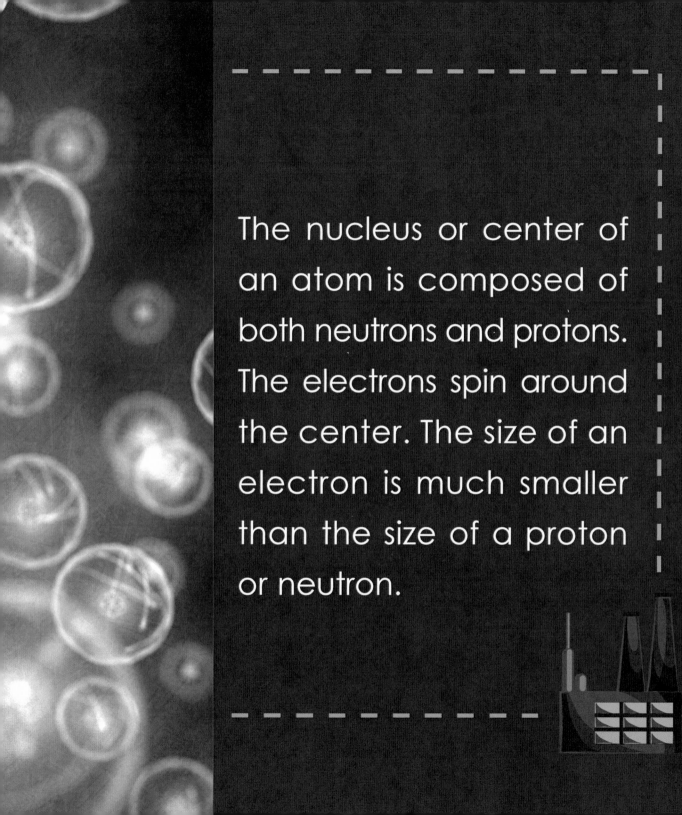

The nucleus or center of an atom is composed of both neutrons and protons. The electrons spin around the center. The size of an electron is much smaller than the size of a proton or neutron.

A proton is about 1,800 times larger than an electron. All the elements in the periodic table have atoms made up of protons, neutrons, and electrons, except for the element hydrogen. Hydrogen doesn't have any neutrons.

Even though atoms are incredibly small there is a huge amount of force inside them.

Hydrogen
(H)

Helium
(He)

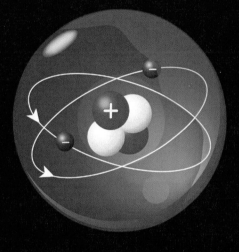

STRUCTURE OF THE ATOMS
HELIUM AND HYDROGEN

WHAT IS NUCLEAR ENERGY?

If you think about the word "nucleus" and the word "nuclear" you will see there is a connection. Nuclear energy is the energy that exists within an atom's nucleus. The amazing amount of power that holds the nucleus of an atom together is called "the strong force."

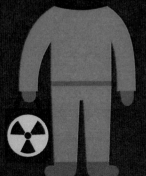

NUCLEAR POWER PLANT

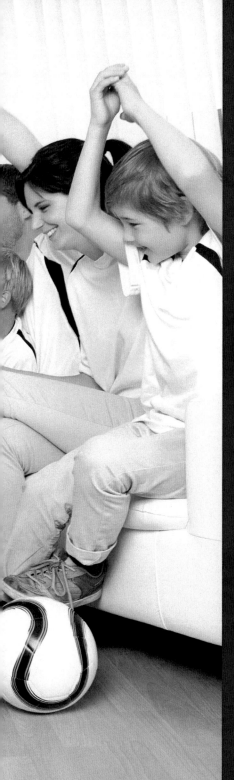

Nuclear energy from nuclear power plants can be used to generate the electricity we need for our homes and manufacturing factories. There are two ways that the energy from the atom can be released—fission and fusion.

ALBERT EINSTEIN'S FAMOUS EQUATION

To understand the process of nuclear fission, you need to know a little about how matter gets converted into energy. The famous physicist Albert Einstein showed the relationship between matter and energy through a formula that almost everyone knows, but few understand. That formula is $E = mc^2$.

ALBERT EINSTEIN

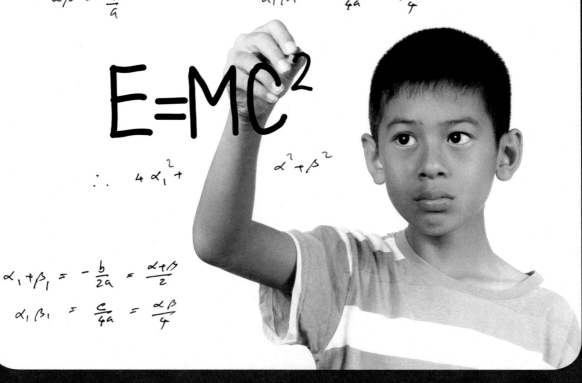

E in this equation stands for energy and m stands for matter. The variable c stands for the speed of light in a vacuum. The speed of light in a vacuum is a very large number—186,282 miles in just one second--and the equation says to square this number so that means multiplying the number by itself.

Einstein's equation basically tells us that a very tiny amount of matter can generate an enormous amount of energy. However, in order for matter to be converted into energy, the atom must be split apart. The process of splitting an atom apart is called nuclear fission.

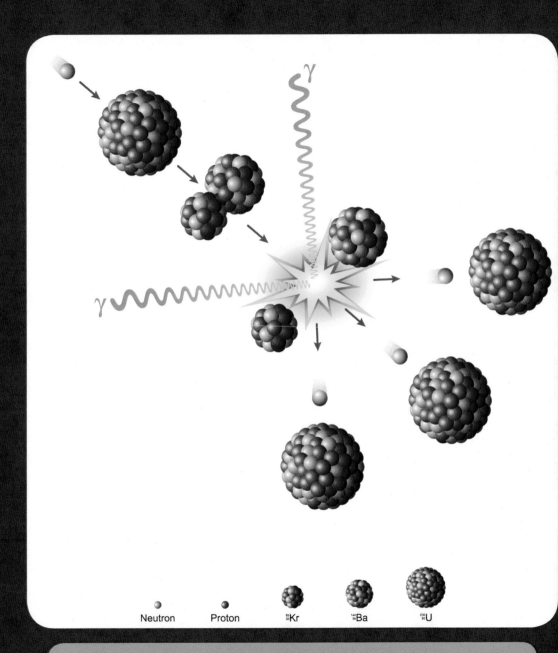

Neutron   Proton $^{89}_{36}$Kr $^{144}_{56}$Ba $^{236}_{92}$U

NUCLEAR FISSION OF URANIUM

POWERFUL EXPLOSION
NUCLEAR BOMB

WHAT IS NUCLEAR FISSION?

When an atom has been split into two or smaller atoms, an enormous amount of energy is generated and nuclear fission has occurred. If the process is controlled and happens slowly, the chain reaction can generate electrical power. However, if the energy isn't controlled properly, it creates an uncontrolled chain reaction, which results in an explosion.

HOW DOES A NUCLEAR POWER PLANT CREATE ENERGY?

The process that nuclear power plants use to create electrical energy from splitting atoms has a series of steps. Within the reactor, a specific type of uranium called uranium 235 is used. Pellets of the uranium are bombarded with neutrons, which force the atoms of uranium to break apart. When they split, they create even smaller particles, which are fission products.

SOLAR PANELS WITH WIND TURBINES AND ELECTRICITY PYLON

WORKER REPAIRS POWERFUL
STEAM NUCLEAR TURBINE

These fission products get a chain reaction started, which causes other uranium atoms to break apart. This reaction generates heat. The reactor contains some type of cooling agent. The cooling agent can be water or molten salt. It can also be a type of liquefied metal. The cooling agent begins to heat up and creates steam.

The steam makes turbines turn. Then, these turbines create the power for generators, which generate the end product of electricity. In order to slow the nuclear reaction down and also to control the amount of electrical energy that's generated, the reactor uses special materials called "nuclear poison."

HUGE INDUSTRIAL HIGH-VOLTAGE
SUBSTATION POWER TRANSFORMER
AT A POWER PLANT

These materials, like the element xenon, soak up some of the fission products, which slows down the speed and force of the nuclear reaction. If the rods are removed, the reaction will be stronger and will generate more power.

Nuclear power plants currently generate about 20% of the power needed for the United States. About 100 plants generate this power.

Most of the US electricity is still generated by renewable hydroelectric power as well as nonrenewable fossil fuels. Worldwide, about 15% of all electrical power is created by nuclear reactors. There are a few nations, such as France and Lithuania, that generate almost all of the electrical power they need from nuclear plants.

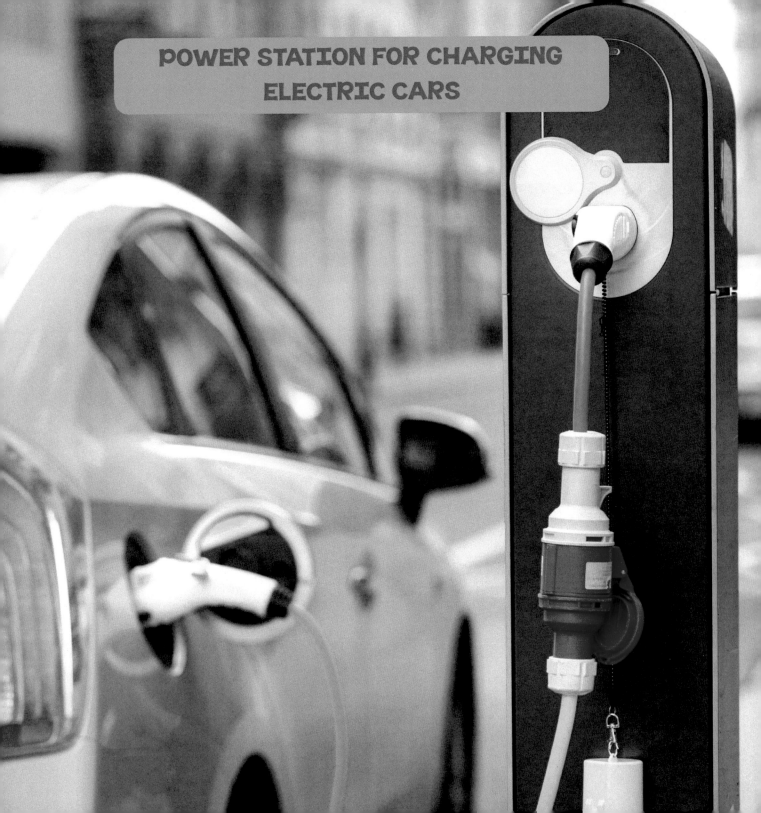

POWER STATION FOR CHARGING
ELECTRIC CARS

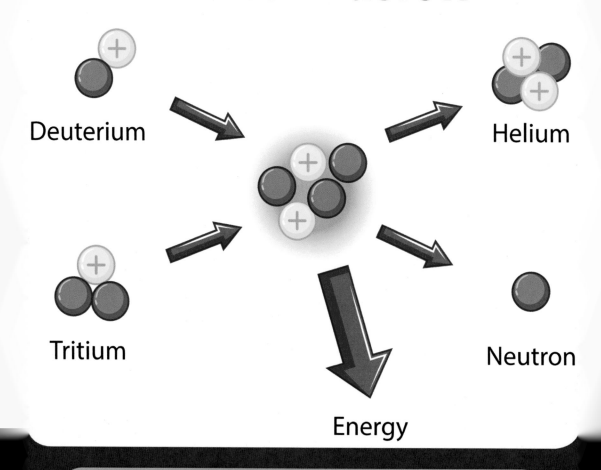

Nuclear Fusion

Deuterium

Tritium

Helium

Neutron

Energy

WHAT IS NUCLEAR FUSION?

Nuclear fission isn't the only way that nuclear energy can potentially be harnessed. Our sun creates nuclear reactions every day when it fuses hydrogen atoms together to create helium. Nuclear fission splits atoms, while nuclear fusion binds them together. The nuclear fusion processes from the sun make life on our planet possible.

SOLAR PANELS AND WIND TURBINES

However, at this time, scientists haven't yet figured out how to create nuclear fusion safely within a power plant so it's not clear if it will be a future option for creating electrical power. It is currently being researched since it would have fewer disadvantages than fission does, because it wouldn't yield as much radioactive waste.

URANIUM 235

The process of creating nuclear energy starts with pellets of uranium as the fuel source. The type of uranium used, U-235, is rare. It makes up only 1% of all the types of uranium available worldwide. The United States mines uranium and also buys uranium from other countries, such as Canada and Russia.

DARK TUNNEL IN OLD URANIUM MINE

A typical reactor uses up to 200 tons of U-235 yearly. Uranium 235 can also be used to create dangerous nuclear weapons. Only nations that have signed a certain treaty that promotes the use of nuclear fuel for peace are allowed to import this type of fuel. Some of the uranium can be recycled for a second use.

IS NUCLEAR ENERGY SAFE?

There are advantages and disadvantages to nuclear power plants. Nuclear reactors create clean energy that is renewable. They give off steam but they don't pollute the air or water with greenhouse gases like fossil fuels do. They can be built near cities or in the country since they don't change the surrounding environment.

WHITE SMOKE OUT OF
INDUSTRIAL SMOKESTACK

ELEMENTARY SCHOOL PUPILS LEARNING ABOUT RENEWABLE ENERGY

The steam produced can be recycled. It can be turned back into water, which can then turn turbines to produce electricity. Any extra steam goes into a smoke stack and is emitted as water vapor that's perfectly safe. However, the process of nuclear energy does create materials that are radioactive. Radioactive material causes the same type of damage as a nuclear explosion.

It can cause severe burns as well as dangerous diseases such as different types of cancer, diseases of the blood, and bone decay. Exposure to large amounts of radioactivity is deadly. The clothing worn by the workers in the plant as well as their tools comes into contact with dust that is radioactive. This type of radioactive waste can stay dangerous for thousands of years.

SCIENTIST CHECKING RADIATION
WITH GEIGER COUNTER

WORKER IN PROTECTIVE UNIFORM, MASK, GLOVES AND BOOTS WORKING WITH BARRELS OF CHEMICALS

The government has to regulate how these types of materials are thrown out because they have the potential to contaminate soil, water, and air. Used uranium pellets as well as the rods used within the reactor have high levels of radioactivity. The storage facilities for these materials have environmental groups very worried.

NUCLEAR ACCIDENTS

There have been three very dangerous accidents involving nuclear power. One was located at Three Mile Island in the United States, one was located at Chernobyl in Russia, and another was located in Fukushima Daiichi in Japan.

Critics of this type of power are worried that the storage facilities for waste that is radioactive will leak and spill dangerous contamination into surrounding soil and water that is underground.

ABANDONED HOUSE INTERIOR IN
CHERNOBYL RESETTLEMENT ZONE

In 1986, at the nuclear plant in Chernobyl, Russia, there was a steam explosion. It caused a radioactive fire that created a plume. Particles that were radioactive fell on the plant as well as the surrounding land.

The radioactive fallout was picked up by the wind and it got absorbed into the water cycle. Radioactivity from the accident spread as far as Ireland and Scotland.

SPECIALIST COLLECTING
SAMPLES FROM A GREEN PUDDLE
OF TOXIC WASTE

PHOTO OF A CHEMICAL WASTE DUMP
WITH A LOT OF BARRELS

It's estimated that the area in the country of Ukraine and the neighboring country of Belarus will be affected for over 3,000 years. Over 100,000 people were relocated as quickly as possible, but the aftereffects of radiation poisoning sometimes take a long time to show up as disease.

Now you know more about the risks and advantages of Nuclear Energy. You can find more Physics books from Baby Professor by searching the website of your favorite book retailer.

Visit

BABY PROFESSOR
EDUCATION KIDS

www.BabyProfessorBooks.com

to download Free Baby Professor eBooks and view
our catalog of new and exciting Children's Books